DECLENSION *in the* VILLAGE *of* CHUNG LUONG

Bruce We

AUSABLE PRESS
2006

Cover art: Greg Elms/Getty Images
Sect motif decoration on the Cao Dai Great Temple, Tay Ninh, Vietnam

Author photo by Kathleen O'Donnell
Design and composition by Ausable Press
The type is Van Dijck with Cicero Titling.
Cover design by Rebecca Soderholm

Published by
Ausable Press
1026 Hurricane Road
Keene, NY 12942
www.ausablepress.org

Distributed to the trade by
Consortium Book Sales & Distribution
1045 Westgate Drive
Saint Paul, MN 55114-1065
(651) 221-9035
(651) 221-0124 (fax)
(800) 283-3572 (orders)

The acknowledgments appear on page 72 and constititute a
continuation of the copyright page.

Library of Congress Cataloging-in-Publication Data

Weigl, Bruce,1949–
Declension in the village of Chung Luong : new poems / Bruce Weigl.
p. cm.
Includes bibliographical references.
ISBN: 1-931337-31-4 (pbk. : alk. paper)
I. Title
PS3573.E3835D43 2006
811'.54–dc22
2006034199

for the dead, etc.

CONTENTS

THREE (where in the seamlessness of all things)

You could have it all
My empire of dirt. . .
—Trent Reznor

TO THE READER

*We are a fast train to nowhere, you and me. We are a swan dive
in search of a cause.*

    *We are a feel-good sleep, deep into your cold morning's flat,
and this is where we leap away,*

        *this is where I piss your name and mine into the midnight snow.
If I wake, expel me, please.*

ONE

(seeing splendid is the door)

THE HEAD OF THE COMPANY

The Head of the company wanted me out. An almost tiny man,
he had come to hate excellence and accomplishment,
and he had made a cult of the same,
who gathered around him like fearful bait fish
around shadow. He wore a grand and flamboyant hat to cover his
baldness, which he suffered badly on other men, especially tall men,
like me, with hair.
          This little man had contrived for himself some little power,
which he used badly, because he was small,
and because he hated his smallness.
I still had faith in those days that the truth mattered,
like breathing matters. Some lies of his I hope I've lost forever.
          I don't forgive the small man his many small cruelties.
When he was fired for refusing to step down,
after his corruption had become intolerable,
even among his acolytes,
he disappeared into his regret, and into the unimaginable loss
he must have felt when his power was gone. He was left
with only his smallness, and with his theories that had grown tired
and out of fashion, and with his great hat, and with the map of his
self-hatred, woven into his skull, and with the wreckage in his wake
of some good lives. Woe is the traveler, lost after dark. Woe
are the spirits who long to come home. That was then.
Even the waves of evil flatten out over time,
until they almost disappear.

ANNA, IN MOURNING

We die and we die so many times and still we want to live. I
looked at the face of death more than once
from the corner of my eye,
and his countenance was always calm and reassuring,
like the old woman who smells of lavender in her sleep and who
dragged me to the funeral home
to pay our respects to dead strangers from her old country.

She made me walk to the casket and its
perfumed, powdered body. I had to open my eyes.
Mr. Death has a face like an angel, because he believes in his work.
When we came home—I must have been four or five—
I laid myself out in the tub of hot water my grandmother
had drawn, and closed my eyes, and pretended that I was dead,
floating there like the boy I'd seen,
killed in a car wreck with his family.

WHAT YOU WOULD DO

When you are handcuffed out of nowhere
in the middle of the bloody foreign airport, what would you do.
Think about what it feels like
to sit back on your hand-cuffed wrists
in the back of a black-and-white; no siren or lights, no talk
from the officers who may or may not love the law blindly.
In a cage one morning and all of one long day I lived,
caught in the splendid optics of the modern police, measuring,
before you know it, how many steps back and forth, and across,
as if walking on a rope bridge, burning over nothing.
They will let down the veil between you and them
so that nothing means what it is, and nothing is what it means.
They will do themselves in different voices.

HOW I LIKE IT

I like it awake and I like it asleep. I like it fresh and I like it old.
I like it wet and I like it to burn. I like it weak and I like it strong.
I like it white and I like it black. I like it dressed
and I like it undressed. I like it hot and I like it cool. I like it gay
and I like it straight. I like it hidden
and I like it open. I like it green and I like it burned brown by sun.
I like it in and I like it out. I like it up and I like it way down.
I like it under and I like it hovering above. I like it to hurt
and I like it when it stops. I like it quiet
and I like it loud. I like it hungry and I like it fed.
I like it hungry, and I like it fed.

I CONFESS TO ENJOYING THE FLESH
OF OUR COUSIN, MR. PIG

       I watched some pigs eat another pig who had died.
       They just ate him.
I was twelve and I rode on the back of a big boy's bicycle
       flat into a funnel cloud that picked us up and threw us
into the ditch. I could hear the pigs squeal behind us. The wind
       was ripping shingles from the barn,
and still they fought each other for the flesh. My

       young father
found us in the blitz of rain and wind, and he carried us to a house.
       Roughly he dried my hair, and shook me
as if he were still not certain I was alive. I
       could not stop thinking about
the pigs, eating the other pig.
My father told me and the big boy, who should have known better

       than to ride us into a yellow sky,
that we could have died in the storm,
but it didn't sink in. Not for a long time. Not until now.
       I don't know what happened to those pigs,
caught in the storm.
Afterwards, I saw some sticks of straw
       driven through a phone pole by the wind. They probably
kept on eating because they were pigs,
until there was nothing left.

WHATEVER

You could be at the air strip on Pongo Pongo, like me,
sitting in the fallen terminal's café,
across from a woman whose ass, like a sweet plum,
every man and many of the women sitting nearby
want to hold in the full of their hands. That's
the way it is in the fast lane; that's the way it is on the road.
Under some heavy stars, bright as my showcase,
I think about how to behave among the ruthless,
and among the betrayers of our faith,
yet nothing redemptive unfolds. Still,
you could be in my shoes, though I would not
load my fleshy baggage upon you,
nor the bullet-torn times,
like a scene from a movie,
but you may have the rivers, alive at night
with dark shapes and mirage.
Something splendid might happen. Whatever.

SAY GOOD-BYE

Say River. Say bloody current. Say not enough rice.
   Say mother and father. Say village bell calling.
Say village drum calling. Say music through the trees

   from someone's lonely radio. Say mango
sliced into the woman's open hands.
   Say rice, steaming just in time. Say paths

worn by the naked feet of lovers. Say lovers
   who must hide in the mango groves,
even to say good-bye.

MY AWARD

     I thought that if I ever won one of those big awards
they give to writers, which includes
     not only a large sum of money, but a fancy dinner
and a ceremony where you're presented with your award,
     and where you're encouraged to say a few words
(but keep it brief) to the many swell people
     gathered for an evening of ambiguity
not all of which would be lost on me.
     I thought that if I ever won, I'd wear a classy outfit,
like the one the monopoly guy wears. I'd have the monocle too,
     and an accent. I'd have things in my pockets, connections
in high places. When I dodged the snipers,
     I would seem to float above the stage.

SELF PORTRAIT AT FIFTY-THREE

There's a fire in the vestry beyond hope.

Don't leave the boat, First Sergeant said.

(When she tangos, I'm insane on the floor.)

Into the sanctuary of trees we marched,
canopy over our heads,

oh la, canopy over our heads.

(Do not call. Do not write. Do not wire. Do not

send an emissary. Do not even think of me.)

You live and you live.

Spirit of the broken banister;

spirit of the mad woman

beating our door with her bloody fists

after everything had come to loss.

Spirit of the man who hanged himself,

doo-da, doo-da.

You live and you live and you know so many things. In the end

I want opera played in the trees, and in the thick underbrush

that you may reach

only where the river is deep,

where the blossoms follow the moving water.

IN LOVE WITH EASEFUL DEATH

That was just now a spirit;
a flicker and then gone
into the dusk of trees at the edge of the party
I can no longer bear witness to.
    In the small pond with its faux waterfall and changing
colored lights,
I feed the imported fish into boredom.
    That was surely a humming bird,
flit of color and then vanished into the trees.
I don't ask anymore what's real, and I told no one
    about the absolutely white rabbit
I watched hop through my vision at the Shawmut T-stop
in Dorchester one midnight. I told no one,
but I caught myself wondering,
and then I stopped.

HOME OF THE BRAVE

First many people died, and then
many other brave people
went to save them, and they died too.
There was a short but stunning moment.
The smoke blacked out the sun. People's noses, mouths and eyes
were filled with the dust
of an incinerated empire. Some faces were streaked with blood;
people picked themselves up and began to walk in a great
migration, like a battalion down the highways empty of traffic,
towards their homes and their televisions.
So much was taken from them, and a hole
had been torn into their world,
that one man hung a thousand flags from his house.
You could not see the windows or the doors. So many flags,
you would think we were American.

PORTAL

In our hallucination, the children are instructed
in the ways of finding shelter
when the rain of our bombs comes down
on their small villages and schools. The children
can identify our planes, and
what our planes can do to them. They

sleep the sleep of weary warriors
beaten down and left for nothing in their lonely deaths
that come so slowly you would wish
your own heart empty of blood.
I watched the people gather in the street
to stop the war that is the war against ourselves,
against the children who practice finding our planes
before they're blown up into dust
nobody sees, but that
makes a sound like the vanquished.

OH NATURE

Today some things worked as they were meant to.
A big spring wind came up and blew down
  from the verdant neighborhood trees,
millions of those little spinning things,
  with seeds inside, and my heart woke up alive again too,
as if the brain could be erased of its angry hurt;
  fat chance of that, yet
things sometimes work as they were meant,
  like the torturer who finally can't sleep,
or the god damn moon
  who sees everything we do
and who still comes up behind clouds
  spread out like hands to keep the light away.

BUSINESS REPLY MAIL
FIRST-CLASS MAIL   PERMIT NO. 1   KEENE NY

POSTAGE WILL BE PAID BY ADDRESSEE

AUSABLE PRESS
1026 HURRICANE RD
KEENE NY 12942-9990

NO POSTAGE
NECESSARY
IF MAILED
IN THE
UNITED STATES

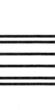

Ausable Press cares what you think about our books. If you have any comments or suggestions, we'd love to hear them.

Title of book: _____

Comments: _____

_____

_____

May we quote you? ☐ Yes ☐ No

☐ Please send me a catalog.

☐ Please sign me up for the Ausable Press e-newsletter.

Name: _____

Address: _____

_____

_____

E-mail: _____

Visit our web site at www.ausablepress.org

NOTHING MORE

The porcelain attitude of the women was merciless
that Saturday.
We were in a cottage by the ocean; the cars were
nineteen and fifty-seven. Oh
the prices of things. Oh the ease with which
we lived with our spirits and with our selves.
The mist around the moon was only that. The wolf
was just a wolf, however at our door. All things
were what they were, and nothing more.

EDDY

My friend Eddy had a younger brother who
definitely had something fucked up in his brain. Eddy's mother
prayed out loud all day in her bedroom, lit with candles.
I never heard his solemn, steel mill father
utter one single syllable. Not ever.

Because no one else would, I loved Eddy. I went to his house
where other children feared to go. I heard his mother
pray and weep so loud, I almost ran away
until Eddy held my wrist and said to take it slow.
I didn't know then what immaculate beauties I was among.

We tried to teach his brother how to use a fork and spoon;
how to zip his fly and pee like a man;
how to swing the bat, but he never learned,
and I didn't know then
that love could be about two boys like that,

or that what Eddy held fast before the waves of prayer,
and the stony father's silence,
and the world's infinite
indignities, is called brother,
and what he gave up, is called everything.

IRAQ DRIFTING, JULY 2003

Listen to me, just for a moment. I have to bother you
with a story about how it feels when the dead speak to me.
I want to annoy you with the facts.
They press their faces against the inside of a glass bubble.

They press their faces
against some kind of net, or web
of dim light, and ask of me favors, and call me friend. This
feels like the loneliness of fireflies

who rise and rise for love until they surrender
to the last darkness. This
feels like the urn, emptied of its oil for the last time. No mercy.
No tongues cut out. No dumb fucks. No democracies.
No dead bodies any more.

WORDS FOR CALVIN
in memoriam

You were headed into the earth that I imagined was warm,
just having been opened up that way, so for a moment
I wanted you to not be in your worldly clothes, but
naked to the warm earth
that must have wanted you on your way,

but the night you died, I did not want to let you go
when your eyes rolled into what looked like death. I tried

to breathe you back. I thought you couldn't have gone
that far so quickly,
but my breath wasn't any good for you, and not my weak pounding
on your chest, until Mary of the house
took me by my arm and told me it was time to let you go,
and so I did, and that was that; soon enough for the rest of my life.

CON GAI BO

Amazing that you're not afraid, even when the night holds
such touching shadows as these,
      in the way we make them, in our minds.
That you would interrupt my short time alone,
      my hour of recovery before spiritual death,
is funny to me, but here you are, in your bright
      pajamas we bought in Hanoi,
the words misspelled in English across the front,
      and in your black eyes, the rivers of Binh Luc
still churn and swell and twist to the great sea of your coming.

I wanted to say that you were my river,
or that you were my flower, or that you were my yellow bird,
      but I didn't want the words to hold you down
the way words do. I didn't want the words
      to bend you,
so I kept quiet. I watched you
      —do you remember?—
as you squatted by the fish pond
      and dragged a stick across your reflection.
Way back in another time,
      to a memory of the green place we
sometimes may not name, I watched you.

TWO

(burn, shining body, quickly make tongues, this no where)

HANOI DRIFTING, JANUARY 2003

You can follow the stolen avenue's emblem
to where the cyclo lifts away, just beyond the barges,
and be nowhere before you pray.

How quickly your tongue goes mute as you bend down
to drink from the stream on a limestone boulder
until the god relents, and the memory lets go too,

through the cells and up the long ganglia,
with all of the family gathered,
and the rolls of sinew burning on a few white coals.

THE BURNING OIL RISES THROUGH THE WICK

      The witches have grown tired of my door, so I
breathe a little easier. The trick is not to be so satisfied
      with more and more of everything
that feeds a grievous hunger.
      You may meet the knife that wants your heart,
or some river that calls you to wade the deep holes;
      and stand on the edge of an ancient fault
that may or not ever bottom out.

MOON OF THE RED GRASS

. . . and young we were in relation to the singers of our time,
and then later, we were young like love
      turned loose in the stream, like
money and her enzymes, all of this against a blue sky back-drop.
You and me, legendary crazy, but gone now
      to lose the madness over mountains;
moon of the red grass, baby.

KINGDOM

 Plaintive evening bird song, summer half away from us. Our
nation's Independence Day; we live inside a war
  made from the liar's chair, made from the chairs
of the brokers of lives,
  so it's only right
a thunderstorm should sweep down on us
  a brief rain, but fresh and cool.

Then fireworks across the sky, and my face and body
  cringed at some louder charges, beyond my control.
Such a night for creatures in the back yard trees
  who have no use for us, or for our celebrations.
They have a shining body each to each, lit by bursting bombs
  that make a shape in the air like a kingdom.

THE STAKES AS HANDS

The stakes that the surveyors laid to mark the boundaries
of my land still stand above the drifted snow, as if someone
outstretched a hand to strangers who may pass my house.
Another war is waiting on the line to start; so many
we will send to die, and tonight
the snow is general all through the city:
an almost vast unfolding into tundras of our loneliness.
Yet it's only snow. The stakes are stakes, not hands that reach
to strangers who may pass my house or not.

UNDER ARCTURUS

The three-headed dog waited for me in the rain
       in the form of the father, son, and holy ghost,
all of them once removed in my mind
       from the almost saintly Anna of Jlubiana,
matriarch of the cult of Mary in the St. Vitus church
       of my first and my last communion,

or was it that torn flesh I was exposed to,
       that farmer in Bong Song;
does anyone remember
       how he was cut in half?
I piss under Arcturus, because I'm a free man, and because I'm not.

THE ABANDONMENT OF BEAUTY
AT ALLEN MEMORIAL HOSPITAL

When the polite, almost noiseless doctors
invited Mr. Death into our conversation, my heart sang out.
Not from their words,
because words make you accountable;
they said it with their grim countenance,
and with the weight of their bodies in the space we shared.
I could see Mr. Death
appear in a corner of the midnight window,
and though he would not come into the light,
I knew he had his eye on me.
Oh where was beauty when I needed it.
How it turned away;
how it had loved me through my life like no one else,
then in the end meant nothing.

FOR YOU

You don't know you love me. You whose head
I want to lay my hands on.
You don't even know how I love you: when the river is high,
I love you, or when the river is low down in the mud.
In a time when angels stood among us, our memory was
opened up to a road that led to this worthless, faithless now.

Lonely rivers like us flow out to the sea. Oh
what is that longing in the window, and
how can I feel your blood in mine,
though you don't even know me. You don't even
know my name. You can't even hear me. You can't see me
standing here, my fingers making a flower between us.

ELEGY FOR BIGGIE SMALLS

    Mad bullets crack through the limousine windows
at the corner of bad and mad the saddest day when big men fall
        how they recall the bullet torn morning
the bass so high to die that way
        is not music but you may use it in your mind you may find

the beat there the thing that slips away there'
        no one stays at the edge too long there's no song
that can keep you or defeat you no one to beseech you
        to step back from the edge when you're Big.

MEDITATION AT PENFIELD

Out of my window, winter is presenting its credentials:
beyond doubt, the frozen Robin says from his frozen branch;
yet we love this particular time of death,
the way we love the promise

of each other's lives as sacrifice for our own:
the necessary death so things can grow again.
The world is getting smaller as I speak;
a little more melts away, every day.

MY GOD (WAS ALWAYS OVER ME)

i.
Some bulbs that came up late below the unexpected
      winter sun
are trapped inside a version of themselves
      as they were never meant to be.
I'm tempted in my middle age
      to dance around the pit,
but god was always over me; my god was always over me.

ii.
      Our town dying of winter, the gray sky
turns darker; the sun isn't real at all;
      not at all,
and there's the human nightmare too,
      the blue around the eyes, the sallow brow,
the sour kiss that may not ever come again.

MY UNCLE RUDY IN SUNLIGHT

Out of the hole my father and his brother had dug
below the drainage tiles of my uncle's barn,
        hundreds of mice streamed.
These brothers had dug the hole,
        then snaked a hose deep into the nest the mice had made,
and no way out but one. They had started getting bad,
        and when my aunt found them in her pantry, well,
something had to be done. I was five years old, and I
        stood behind these brave men and watched
between their legs as the mice began to come:
        first, only a few, shaking the water from their fur, blinded
momentarily in sunlight, and then, may I say, a flood of mice;
        more mice than anyone had expected, even I knew that.
My uncle had a hoe, and my father ran for the rake,
        and you know what happens next.

This was fifty years ago, and I don't know
what business it thinks it has here, in this life, now.
        Yet in the dizzying span of memory,
that morning in the country of mice is as clear to me
        as my own face, which I love,
and as clear as the face of my uncle,
        moving in and out of the blinding sun as he raised the hoe,
and then came down hard, and then raised the hoe again.

IN HAI PHONG

In Hai Phong I shared my hotel room with a friend
from Hanoi. He lay on the floor by my bed;
     in the dark, he told me

     how he once had his mouth
pressed against the tangle of a woman's sexual hair,
     and then he said her name out loud—Hoa,

which means flower.
     He said that the flower of her sex
opened when he said her name, his lips

     pressed against her lotus lips.
My friend told me this story
     without irony, and with a sweetness men where I come from

mostly don't understand. The noisy fan
     almost kept time with the rhythm of his words. The heat,
even at midnight, was unbearable. I heard

shouts out in the street, and a woman laughing. My
     friend said that when the lights went out, she put her
fingers inside his mouth.

DOCTRINE OF TWO TRUTHS

In the middle of the doctrine of two truths, my nose fills
with the smell of soup (I wanted to say death?)
It is the soup my daughter makes
when she thinks about her village in the rain;
the soup of yesterday's rice, tomato, and fatty beef
sliced thin the way not having teaches. I can't see
but I know she tends it with her deft chopsticks,
and she understands when it's right,
then she calls me in to eat.

I had been trying to make the real and the not real
absent from my mind, but the smell of the soup would not let me
from concepts be free; would not leave me in peace.
Soup of the mother of the other life, and of a family
that is a village
etched into her mind
and into the rhythm of her walk,
as she walks away.

DEAD MAN, THINKING

i.

      Snow geese in the light of morning sky,
exactly at the start of spring. I was
      looking through the cracks of the blinds at my future
          which seemed
absent of parades, for which I was grateful,
      and only yesterday

I watched what an April wind could do
      to a body wrapped in silk,
though I turned my eyes away,
      the way the teacher says,
once the beauty was revealed.

ii.

How long it takes to die, in the fifty-fifth year
      is what I thought about today.
I told some truths so large, no one could bear to hear them.
      I bow down to those who could not hear the truth.
They could not hear the truth because they were afraid
      that it would open a veil into nothing.
I bow down to that nothing. I bow down to a single red planet
      I saw in the other world's sky,
spinning,
      as if towards some
fleshy inevitability.

      I bow down to the red planet. I bow down
to the noisy birds, indigenous to this region.
      Only sorrow can bend you in half
      like you've seen on those whose loves have gone away.
I bow down to those loves.

THE PRISONER OF OURS

      I don't know why the dove should be so lonely
this early in spring, but all this cloudy day long
      he's called out lonely cries from the willow
beside the garden where I work. Then I thought

      it must have been some gods grieving for our naked prisoner,
set upon by the exquisitely trained military dogs. He's
      bleeding on the concrete floor below a female soldier
who taunts him with what can only be called glee.

      The grieving dove sounds like a last plea to no one
for some peace.
      Because she loved her son, the mother of our prisoner
begged for us to kill him, to save him from the shame and

      humiliation that was, in her belief, worse than death.
But death cannot have him, and his mother cannot have him,
      and not the snarling dogs, because he is ours; he is
our prisoner, and he will always be ours.

PATRICK, IN MEMORY

We were stepping large and laughing easy,
        out on the night in some New York mountains
that happened to be black and drowsy with deer in summer,

then the car is rolling over and across a ditch,
        then comes to rest just in the moon, and the sweet boy,
whose life we had come to celebrate, sat dazed, crunched

by the caved-in car top, his neck broken, his hands and his legs
        gone forever.
I kneeled beside him in the trees when he screamed

he couldn't move his body, he couldn't breathe. I knew
        that a weight had been
humped up onto our backs, to carry with us through the days

        we had left. When bad things happened in the war,
things you couldn't bear to see, or even think about,
        we used to say: It don't mean nothing.

BEFORE YOU TURN AWAY

I traveled in the land of women, and lord I lost my way.
I have no excuse, though I have never liked to say
no, or good-bye.
No one wanted to ruin anyone else in those days,
not as far as I can remember,
and such and such, and la de da,
and oh the fool I was,
and how desperate is the breath, stolen from the other's lips
in the evening light of grim motels, and
how much sweat soaked longing does it take
before you finally turn away. It's not living.
It's not living.

THREE

(where in the seamlessness of all things)

THE FIRST FATHER-MURDERED RABBIT

The smell of the rabbit's blood in the back of my father's
chevy from more than fifty years ago
      comes back to me today,
out of a tunnel of some kind
is the best I can do
      to explain what I mean. The smell of the rabbit's blood
had been inside of me all along; (I am most alive
inside of words, and most safe in their aisles of fancy.)

      That boy didn't have to see the rabbit, pearl of blood
at the tip of its nose,
but he did, and he didn't have to help skin the rabbit clean,
      but he did that too, at his father's side.
      You don't know at the time
just what it is that you're getting yourself into;
      just what doors
you may open, and then never come back.

DECLENSION IN THE VILLAGE
OF CHUNG LUONG

> The dark is so dark in the northern countryside.
No city lights, few
> > cars, mostly oil lamps and small fires for cooking,
by which you may see the faces of living people.
> > In the afternoon, I had watched some small boys
bathe and swim and play
> > in the clay-colored water of this village pond,
where only they may swim, and never a girl.
> > Beyond the pond,
beyond the three churches in the village, beyond the school,
> > and the teacher's house, beyond the endless fields of rice,
the river valley opens up into a kingdom
> > whose river is as red as the patriots' blood.
Red as the blood of the comrade,
> > dead where she waited for her lover
in the mango grove;
> > dead by the hand of the puppet soldiers
who shoot in the back
> > so you may not see their face. Loss
is a red thread, woven into the cloth of the woman's shawl; grief
> > is the knot that binds it.

DEPARTING GALWAY

On a ferry out of Galway on Loch Corrib, on our way to the old
school house and its child-like spirits,
  to hear some Irish poets, but half a crossing later,
a storm came up quick and hard, so the captain, crew of one,

  labored to make our landing place, though nothing doing,
and he wouldn't try it more than once he said; he said
  that was for fools and drowned sailors, and he
turned us back into the wind, and steered us through a pounding,

  gladdening rain towards home and our Galway port,
where some strangers waited on the dock
  that I thought might have been
ghosts the way you could walk through them,

  but before that,
along the way in the storm,
  we huddled together on the covered deck and listened
to the old words again,
  and the words were written in the water
churned up white and cresting,

  and they were written across the sky
when some lightning flashed,
  and the words were written on the faces of fishermen
who ignored the storm and hunkered down to wet a line,
  and they were written all across the green hills of Galway,
and across the vales and the stream beds,
  a great wall of words that you could finally claim as your own.

WHAT THE MARTYR SAID

After the woman and her kid got onto the T without paying,
    another woman approached her,
who was sitting by now, her still-sobbing child
    held between her legs as the train started up
then bucked and shook, then started up again.
    The woman crossed the aisle between them
and was saying something to the weary mother,
    and though I couldn't quite hear over the noise,
it was clear that she was letting her have it good,
    even pointing her finger in the woman's face,
and then as we all watched, the mother raised up
    and leaned into the face of the uninvited woman,
and her opinions, and screamed

    You don't know me. You don't know who I am.
Why the fuck do you think I have to
    sneak onto this fucking train with my kid, you bitch?

The pointing finger woman; the one you might call
    a good citizen, was drained of color now,
as if her entire life had somehow come down to this single
    unastonishing moment. It was the end of a long day.
The baby was still crying, afraid
    of his mother's shouts. There was a short pause.
She reached into her bag, and then she said the word gun.

THE ONE THOUSANDTH

We watched the one thousandth dead soldier's face
on the color television with a flat screen so that
no matter where you sat, you saw him face to face.
With the promise of the liars on his lips,
he died in the liar's war. To die alone in the desert,
far from home, far from the people who love you,
is not ever a glorious thing, and I don't give a fuck
what my government says otherwise. Sacrifice and slaughter
are not the same things. The sorrowful red star mothers
will come out of their houses to tell you that
in the thousand languages, the thousand cities,
and the thousand torn hearts,
and what do we say to them,
and what do we say to the faces we see in our own mirrors,
the ones who still want answers, even as we turn away.

LESSON FROM DA LAT

We love emptiness
because reason is useless.

The boy carries his cricket in a box his grandfather
had constructed with heart-breaking

care from tiny splinters of bamboo.
He carries it in his satchel with the ball of sticky rice

his mother had wrapped for him in a banana leaf, for his lunch,
in the still dark morning while he slept.

He walks to school
with his friends through the mango trees,

the guardians of wandering beings
everywhere.

LATE SUMMER LILIES

I kiss the late summer lilies because they want me to,
and how do you say no to lilies
        dying of beauty you can barely stand to see.
I don't know if I heard a voice or not, or anything at all,
        except the dangerous wind. Nothing else to say

        in this great Republic of Voices, this Republic of Lies.
Into the darkness to see I was called,
        and to taste the salty flesh,
and to suck sweet juice from the lilies, holes in the sky
        moving away from us like nothing we've ever seen.

I DON'T KNOW HOW MUCH MORE

my heart can take of sorrow, and of the trouble of others,
especially the trouble, and heartache, and suffering,
and the loneliness of others
who have always been drawn to my life.
        Just last night I watched a starving child
try to spoon boiled rice into her mouth,
only her arms were too weak to lift the spoon.
        I don't want the weight of anybody on my back anymore
is how I feel when I look around these days. I don't want to watch
the sky move past everyday, but I do, and I don't want to love
        words so much, but I do, and I don't want to know
why it is that your heart is broken, but you'll tell me.
That's the way it goes on a good day.
        Nothing but blue skies.

HONEY

I love it when you call me honey.
        I love it when I make you laugh out loud in public,
and the sound your laughter makes

is an old song by now, and you and me
        are an old song by now,
like my last and ancient good-bye

to you, my one great love,
        and to the green trees outside my window
in the last of summer's warm light,

and to the loyal shadows.
        I don't want a different life.
I want the life where the moon is bright on the still pond,

and the mountain's worn smooth
        by the palm of a woman's hand.
I want the life where I wait for you in dark rooms,

for the shape of you, that I know like nothing else,
        to appear beside to me, and then your hand on my back,
my fierce and only wonder, my anchor.

BAD INTERVIEW

I lie beside a woman all night,
listen to her story of her lover's suicide;
how he'd managed to squeeze off two rounds into his own heart;
how he couldn't bear the loss of his lie.
This was in the apartment my friend was sharing
with the wife of her dead lover, in the months after his death,
perhaps to try to understand.
She talks all night, and I listen, and then she calls me
up to her bed and under her covers where we sleep
a few fitful hours. I am cold, and her small body is warm,
until I hear some traffic start up outside, still dark and December,
and I dress to leave without waking her.
(I have an interview at eight across town
and no money for a taxi so I walk to my hotel.)
On the cold, four a.m. street of dress shops,
I turn a corner, glimpse someone, and
something's wrong my body says,
so I pick up my pace. No one on the a street, but I can
hear him behind me, and turn to see him pass under the street light.
He is huge, with a huge head tied with a babushka,
and he wears thick makeup, smeared across his lips and eyes, and
red rouge smeared all down his cheeks.
He wears a woman's coat which comes open when he walks so I can see
he has on nothing else except for shoes, no socks.
I pick up my pace, and when I come to another corner,
I begin to run, until I think I must be out of his reach,
and I stop to catch my breath a block from my hotel. I try to breathe
cold air until I hear him almost on me again. I'm
tired. I want to stand and fight, or do whatever I have to do
to put this thing to rest, whatever it is, whatever divine test or
Pavlovian training regime for the mad, I want to get to it,
but when I see his face again in the light, and his cock
hanging out of his open coat, I start to run hard,

and make some distance on him fast,
round the final corner, open the outer door, and unlock the inner
just as the she-man arrives outside. On the glass door he beat his fists
when he finds that it's locked. I stand there,
braced against the front desk with the terrified night clerk,
and watch the man smash his face against the glass,
smearing his makeup, saying something neither of us can hear or
understand. He beats so hard on the door that others began to gather.
He pounds on the door and tries to say something.
People watch him through the glass, as if he were TV,
strangers in their pajamas, and me,
already slinking down the hall to my room
on the umpteenth floor, and my door with its double locks,
and my windows which I look out of and see him
still standing there, pounding on the door,
still calling something out, and then looking up at me.

APOLOGY TO NO ONE, NOVEMBER SEVENTEENTH, TWO THOUSAND FOUR

I didn't stop to consider the sociological implications
before I acted, or before I spoke out.
Someone at the academic party said "vis à vis" and I lost it;
I fell into a beautiful flashback, man,
rockets that sound like trains through the night sky, but
that was that, more or less instantaneous, so that no one noticed
I had left and then come back. You
don't have to tell me a thing or two about portals,

I've seen the visitors come and go.
There's the talk, and then there's the talk about the talk.
And isn't this romantic, to love words and the sounds of words,
even as the bodies pile up in secret; even as the children
are terrorized out of their minds by bombs we pay for. You can only
cover your mouth, so you won't scream out loud.

COYOTE NEAR THE HANFORD ROAD BRIDGE

How can you ignore the dead coyote,
     mostly curled up
gold and black in the grassy ditch.
     You stop and back up
to where its beauty lies
     magnificent, unreachable to you
through the mind of its wildness.
     You want to say that you stayed a long time,
but you didn't. You found no ritual there,
     though you let yourself fall
as deep as you could into that coyote's heart.
     You had been lucky to come across his still warm body
in the dark near the Hanford Road bridge. You were drunk
     from too much good wine,
already forgetting conversations you'd had
     only moments before, with people who love you.
You were driving too fast in the night
     away from that love, away from anything
you imagined could save you.
     You had pictured your own blaze of glory. You wanted to
wrap your car fast around something that would not give, but
     how can you ignore the coyote,
curled up into the night ditch
     like a god. Pull over brother. Take a few deep breaths.

NOTES FROM A CONVERSATION WITH BECKIAN

One could say that obsession is a world view,
or a technique, like
    bent over the sink before the unlying mirror
is a technique.
    The way we use the word "amplify,"
to say what we really mean is
    expand; the way they wanted me
to amplify my responses
    to their questions in the airport deemed unsafe by many.
Or the way that we may
    amplify our obsessions to the degree
that they are no longer visible to anyone,
    or I could say:
Get out foul words. Get out all leper evangelists.

MY SECOND WINTER COYOTE

An aloneness can come over me when I'm driving at night
so I feel like someone's inside the car with me,
        and last night he wanted to show off and so
pushed down hard on one of my thighs,
        out on a frozen road I love to drive,

and he showed me the second coyote, this one
        more alive than light, and more quick
than any eye can move
        to keep him in sight; yet he stops
in the car's light to watch
        what I would do next; he counts his escapes
before he makes a single move, and plots with his eyes
        such a quick red rush.

BY WAY OF ELEGY, FOR MY FRIEND
(*Corporal Paul Cook, Retired, U.S. Army, in memoriam*)

A little white light off the frozen snow this morning
      when some sun came through the clouds,
but was gone then, like a doe on scent of danger;
      like a day is gone. Winter's so long

because we count the days, and measure their
      propensity for tragedies of ice or snow or
blowing, frozen wind across the lake. First
      there is the dying, right before your eyes.

READING THE GUARDIANS OF THE LOTUS SUTRA, AN OLD FRIEND COMES BACK TO ME

I could not have imagined that wrenching dot of time:
our lives separating like streams one day,
    there and then gone,
but in my mind, I have seen you standing in water,
    if I may be so excused to say,
and I have seen you running in high grass too,
    and being in love with your life.
What comes back to me in the cold
    is that something bound us for awhile,
so tightly I thought I'd lost myself
    somewhere inside of you, and was glad for that.
I who have loved you all this time.
    I who found the earrings in the snow.
(Sister, sister smash these earrings
    off against the tree you said
and then you ran away.)

    Cold in the portico of the Romanesque, I found you,
though I didn't know what to do.
    You gave me back a joy I thought I'd never have again.
You made the movie stop sometimes, with just your smile.
    I wanted you so badly
I had to put my arms around
    the beauty that you were inside that chance of light,
and that you are,
    as I have imagined you
every day of my life,
    grown older in that beauty, and strong,
where you were always strong.

In the mind, such a crushing thing doesn't matter,
though I wanted to say the words of you,
        the climbing up the wall for you;
your black hair I could drown inside,
        the cotton dress we both took off
to the sea of your olive skin.
        We think we have it down.
We think we have it all figured out.
        I wanted your wings to wrap around me
in the city where you were
        lovely on the bus where I waited.
I would wait for you that way.

LE FILME

    I hear the screams of children
blown to pieces by bombs
    guided precisely to a room
in the house next door
    where a "target" lived, or
didn't; that kind of thing.

The deaths pile up
    as if on my shoulders;
this is no metaphor;
    the pile grows and grows.
We can't keep up with the names anymore.
I am pulled inside the war. I am pulled inside the war.
    Nothing I can do
can stop even one fucking death; not one.
The film is black and white,
    and one day will be "lost."

POOR EXCUSE

You said the word *exotic* so it sounded like New York,
it sounded like a plea for something slightly dangerous,
the way these matters are sometimes,
and at the same time, it sounded like something different,
the opposite of dangerous: safe, only with some happiness there too.
It was how you said the word into the cold Parisian air
that makes all of the difference; the way the word
fell off of your tongue and lips, and was carried, up and away
on the frozen strands of your breath.
We try and try
but the word can never be the thing,
and only nothing comes, only my
highly suggestible nerves in fits of lonely laughter come. I am
open to the raw sky. I am spinning planet and solo flight. I am
sacrifice, and poor excuse.

MEDITATION ON SCOUT MASTER BILL

The memory frightened out of me by the sheer thing itself;
        the events, the equipment, and the protocol,
all slightly off key by now, but it was
        the Boy Scouts of America,
and the master was a guy named Bill who loved his beer.
        We strapped on our gear and
hiked three miles to our campsite
        and with night coming so fast, I stayed as close as I could
which took my breath away
        until I heard a river rush,
and Bill tell us all to stop.
        In the dark he walked off the shape of a campsite
and we began to set up tents. First
        is master Bill's, with its own generator,
eight inch black and white TV, and electric plugs
        to make popcorn, or heat up dogs;
nobody dared to go there. We were
        tired once we'd set up camp.
We crawled into our sleeping bags and tried to go to sleep,
        though we were lonely too,
and the air already cool enough to make it hard to fall asleep.
        Things went quiet.
I could hear the popping and cracking sound of a big fire, dying,
        and the sound of master Bill, laughing at his TV.
I close my eyes again and fall
        deep into that drowsy numbness
that's not sleep but
        that's not *not* sleep either; the in between where you may
travel if you wish to lay it on the line. I fell asleep
        because of his whispered, drunken voice in my face. The brilliant
things I kept in mind

when he got up on the cot: my scout knife
in my pocket, my scout ax next to my bunk. What words can do
        is not anything at all; not anything. He fell asleep drunk,
his drunk mouth in my face,
        more than once
on that first and last trip with troop 127.
        He fell asleep drunk in my cot; the details here
become unimportant, the focus on the horizon
        no longer an issue.
He emptied his half-full bottle of beer over my head.
        First it was cold
and then it was warm, and then you imagine
        what's next in this ritual.
I loved the Boy Scouts of America.
        I loved their rules and their codes you had to memorize,
and the uniform could fit so nicely,
        and I loved Scout Master Bill like the river loves the rocks.
I am swift like the river,
        and move easily around the rocks.
I am strong like the rocks,
        unmoved by the constant water.

THIS NO WHERE

This is just a picture that we live inside,
white house, black shutters
frozen snow on the roof and on the ground.
This is just a movie we imagine is our lives, silent transfers
here and there in our cars, to appointments we must keep
or else die a little in someone's estimation; die a little in
someone's head. That's what I think. That's the way I think about it,
and I am only just a little afraid of letting go
completely of knowing anything,
letting go of knowing anything at all,
so I don't know why
we fret so over the loss of beauty, over the passing, or over the death
of beauty, but we do. We try to possess beauty with our lying eyes
and think we know what beauty is or does, and it's a crying shame
what happens to us then.

MY GOOD-BYE

The mermaids do not sing for anyone,
not even for themselves. They sing because they do; because the wind
blows through them
in a way that makes them call out what sounds like desire. We
only imagine that they sing for us

so that we may have someone
to blame when we crash into the rocks. White birds
you called the egrets
from the bridge on Hampton Roads. All those white birds like
the dead come back from their green dying
inside the perfectly shaped bodies of egrets.

We wanted to see the splendor we could feel,
so we drove the rental car
out into a virgin stand of hemlock trees,
the dusk like lace curtains, settling. The dogs
in my mind I live among. That's my good-bye.

NOTES & ACKNOWLEDGMENTS

"Con Gai Bo" is Vietnamese for "father's daughter."

"Say Good-bye" is for Nguyen Phoung, with thanks for her kindnesses.

"Hanoi Drifting" is for Le Lu.

"In Hai Phong" is for Nguyen Quang Thieu, in friendship.

"What the Martyr Said" is for Larry Heinemann, and Riley.

"Patrick, in Memory" is in memory of Patrick Biber.

"Declension in the Village of Chung Luong" is for Nguyen Ve.

"Bad Interview" is for C.D. Wright and her lovely mind.

"By Way of Elegy, For My Friend" is for Don Cook.

"Notes From a Conversation with Beckian" is for Beckian Fritz Goldberg, with gratitude for her inspiration.

"My Goodbye" is for J.C., in memoriam.

Grateful acknowledgment for their generous support is given to the editors of the following magazines, in which some of these poems first appeared:

The American Poetry Review: "Iraq Drifting, July 2003," "The Head of the Company," "What You Would Do," "I Confess To Enjoying the Flesh of Our Cousin, Mr. Pig," "Self-Portrait at Fifty-Three," and "Home of the Brave."

Hunger Mountain: "The Burning Oil Rises Through the Wick," "The Stakes as Hands," and "Hanoi Drifting, 2003."

Irish Pages: (Belfast): "Anna, in Mourning," "How I Like It," "Whatever," "My Award," "In Love With Easeful Death," "Nothing More," "Eddy," "Say Good-bye," "How I Like It," "Con Gai Bo," "Portal," and "Oh Nature."

The Georgia Review: "The One Thousandth," "What the Martyr Said."

Michigan Quarterly Review: "Doctrine of Two Truths"

Sentence: "Before You Turn Away," and "Patrick, in Memory."

The Kenyon Review: "Moon of the Red Grass," "Kingdom," "For You," "My Uncle Rudy in Sunlight," and "In Hai Phong."

Whiskey Island: "Apology To No One, November Seventeeth, Two Thousand Four," "The Abandonment of Beauty in Allen Memorial Hospital," "I Don't Know How Much More," "The First Father-Murdered Rabbit," and "By Way of Elegy, for My Friend."

(My gratitude also to Dr. Mark Luciano, for saving my brain.)